# 20TH CENTURY USA

# History
## *of the*
# 1920s

Rennay Craats

**WEIGL PUBLISHERS INC.**

Published by Weigl Publishers Inc.
123 South Broad Street, Box 227
Mankato, MN, USA   56002
Web site: http://www.weigl.com

Library of Congress Cataloging-in-Publication Data available upon request
from the publisher. Fax (507) 388-2746 for the attention of the Publishing
Records Department.

ISBN 1-930954-09-3

Printed and bound in the United States of America
1 2 3 4 5 6 7 8 9 0   06 05 04 03 02

**Senior Editor**
Jared Keen

**Series Editor**
Carlotta Lemieux

**Copy Editor**
Jay Winans

**Layout and Design**
Warren Clark
Carla Pelky

**Photo Research**
Joe Nelson

**Photograph Credits**

American Stock/Archive Photos: page 23, 29; APA/Archive Photos: pages 6BL, 33; Archive Photos: pages 6BR, 10, 16, 18, 19, 21, 22, 24, 42, 43; Bettmann/CORBIS: pages 7BL, 8, 9, 15, 39B; Camera Press Ltd./Archive Photos: pages 37; CORBIS: page 32; Hulton-Deutsch Collection/CORBIS: page 34; Minnesota Historical Society/CORBIS: page 27; National Archives of Canada: pages 3TR(RD00805), 36(RD00805), 38(C36148); New York Times Co./Archive Photos: page 14; Photofest: pages 3TL, 11, 12, 13, 28, 30, 31T, 31B, 40T, 40B, 41B; Popperfoto/Archive Photos: pages 3B, 6BR, 17, 20, 25, 26, 35.

Every reasonable effort has been made to trace ownership and to obtain permission to reprint copyright material. The publishers would be pleased to have any errors or omissions brought to their attention so that they may be corrected in subsequent printings.

# USA 1920s Contents

**Entertainment** 10

**Literature** 24

**Fashion** 36

Wall Street Shakes

Bloody Sunday

Steamboat Willie

PROHIBITION

Lenin Dead

King Tut's Tomb

Mah-jongg Mania

Oscar Arrives

Great Gatsby

Women's Suffrage

After World War I ended, Americans were eager for a return to everyday life. They wanted to put the conflict behind them and have a good time. The twenties started off fairly slowly, but the minor economic recession after the war gave way to prosperity. The extra money and shorter work weeks allowed people to relax. Many Americans went to the hottest nightclubs to dance the Charleston and enjoy jazz music. Others played mah-jongg or listened to the radio. Hollywood superstars, including Rudolph Valentino, Buster Keaton, and Mae West, kept the theaters packed to the rafters. Sports fans watched the rise of the incredible New York Yankees and the arrival of a U.S. team in the National Hockey League.

The economy continued to improve. The decade was full of opportunities to make money quickly. Some people invested all they had in the stock market. Others looked for their fortunes in real estate. The boom became

Hollywood Speaks

Crazy for Coco

Boom and Bust

Dam Collapses

Scopes Trial

Harlem Renaissance

Mussolini's Reign

RED SCARE

Silent Cal

a bust in 1929 with the crash of the New York Stock Exchange. The country was plunged into a depression that would last for many years.

*20th Century USA: History of the 1920s* is a fun way to explore the Roaring Twenties. This book profiles accounts of many fascinating events that took

place and the people who made them happen in the twenties. There is much more that happened during this decade than appears on these pages. To find out more about this time in history, visit your local library. It has countless resources that will help you research the twenties. The Internet is also a great

place to learn more about what happened during the 1920s. For now, turn the page and begin your journey through time.

**1920**

For many women, it was a long time coming. They are finally given the right to vote. Find out the reaction to this law on page 20.

**1920**

Wall Street rocks in September. A bomb blast causes chaos in New York. Find out more on page 9.

**1920**

America runs "dry." Prohibition makes it illegal to make or consume alcohol. Learn more about this contested law on page 20.

**1920**

Americans tune in! KDKA airs the first commercial radio broadcast in the country. Discover where the historic event took place and the stir it caused across the country on page 10.

**1921**

Americans are smelling like Coco. Women spray on more Chanel No. 5 than any other perfume. Learn more about this fashion leader on page 37.

**1921**

Parents breathe a little easier due to the work of French scientists. Their vaccine is a solution to one of the most deadly diseases in the world. Find out more on page 27.

**1922**

Howard Carter keeps digging until he finds what he is looking for. His discovery captures headlines around the world. Find out what he unearthed in Egypt on page 16.

**1922**

Hollywood studios are dreaming in color. Their dreams come true with *Toll of the Sea*. Turn to page 27 to learn more about this major change to movies.

**1923**

A development in the White House shocks Americans. The Teapot Dome Scandal ravages President Harding's administration. Find out more on page 21.

**1924**

The U.S. passes restrictive immigration policies. Read more about the limits and exclusions on page 38.

**1924**

Professional hockey travels from Canada to the U.S. The first American team joins the National Hockey League. Page 30 has the scoop.

**1924**

Mohandas Gandhi goes without food in the name of independence. See how the Mahatma's hunger strike helped his country on page 19.

**1925**

Iran's Qajar dynasty is no more, thanks to Reza Khan. Turn to page 18 to find out how he changed iran.

The right to vote

President Harding

**1925**

The Bible goes head-to-head with evolution in Dayton, Tennessee. Page 23 has more about the legendary Scopes Trial.

**1925**

Oxford bags help university students get around the rules. Page 36 has the details on how baggy pants solved fashion questions.

**1925**

Americans "keep cool with Coolidge." They elect "Silent Cal," and the popular president is sworn in. Find out about the campaign and election on page 22.

**1926**

The sun rises on Hemingway. His novel inspires a generation and makes him famous. Turn to page 24 to find out more.

**1926**

The Revenue Act is established to help boost the economy. Many Americans never feel the benefits of this legislation. Find out why on page 35.

**1926**

Not even the Saint Francis Dam could hold the water back. Billions of gallons of water pour out of the dam. Turn to page 8 to find out more about this disaster.

**1927**

Babe Ruth leads the New York Yankees. He sets a home-run record that will stand for more than thirty years. Find out more about the incredible athlete on page 28.

**1927**

Turn up the volume—Hollywood adds sound to movies. Find out who the Jazz Singer was and how sound changed movies forever on page 12.

**1927**

Charles Lindbergh is flying high, and he does so on his own. Find out why this is special and noteworthy on page 26.

**1927**

The Great Mississippi Flood sweeps the U.S. Find out why it happened on page 8.

**1928**

Herbert Hoover gains the support and admiration of the country. Turn to page 23 to find out about the new president and his landslide victory.

**1928**

All eyes are on a mouse, and he is not your run-of-the-mill rodent. Mickey Mouse takes the big screen by storm. Find out more on page 13.

**1929**

President Hoover enacts the original Farm Aid. His Agricultural Marketing Act and the Federal Farm Board ease troubles for a while. Turn to page 23 to find out why these actions created only temporary solutions.

**1929**

For the first year of the awards, there was not much extravagance and no red carpet. Page 11 has more about these now-famous awards.

**1929**

The dreams and bank accounts of many Americans dissolve in October. Page 35, tells how the stock market crash came about and the toll it took on Americans.

Saint Francis Dam

Charles Lindbergh

# Dam Collapse

The Saint Francis Dam was built in 1926 at a cost of $1.3 million. It was built to create an emergency water supply for Los Angeles using the Santa Clara River. The incredible structure stood 175 feet high and 175 feet wide, and it spanned about 15 miles of the San Francisquito Canyon. Everything seemed perfectly planned, but the builders forgot a few things. They did not test the rock base in the valley, and they did not anchor one end of the dam. They realized the mistake too late.

On March 12, 1928, the dam could no longer hold the pressure of the water behind it. After a few days of heavy rains, muddy water began seeping out of the ground. The government agency in charge of monitoring the dam did not take action. Twelve hours

later, the dam burst. The sides of the dam fell and were carried nearly a mile downstream. The center of the dam stood strong, but an 80-foot wave rushed over it and into the valley below. Billions of gallons of water were released. Seventy-five construction workers working at the base of the dam were drowned, but five of their friends were carried on top of the wave

■ When the Saint Francis Dam collapsed, it released 12 billion gallons of water.

like surfers. About 600 homes in Santa Paula, a town below the dam, were destroyed. Damages reached more than $30 million. An estimated 450 people died in the disaster, nearly wiping out the entire population of Santa Paula.

## FLOODS SWEEP MISSISSIPPI VALLEY

■ Starting in August 1926, rain hammered Kansas and Oklahoma. It did not stop until December. The soil could not absorb any more water, so rivers swelled. In April 1927, heavy rains and flooding across the Midwestern states continued to plague the Mississippi Valley. More rain fell in April in the Ohio and Missouri valleys, causing the water level to rise still more along the mighty Mississippi River. By the middle of May, high water had caused the **levees** to crack with the pressure in forty-seven spots. Between 11 million and 18 million acres of land were flooded, drowning hundreds of people. About 750,000 homes were under water and 1.5 million farm animals were killed. About 670,000 people were left homeless. Parts of seven states were flooded from April straight through to August. The Great Mississippi Flood was worse than all other Mississippi floods combined. The secretary of commerce at the time, Herbert Hoover, called the flood the "greatest peace-time calamity in the history of the country."

## Wall Street Shakes

The corner of Wall and Broad streets in New York was the money center of the country. The area was home to such businesses as the Sub-Treasury Building, the Stock Exchange, and the U.S. Assay Office. Around noon on September 16, 1920, Manhattan's financial district shook. A bomb had been hidden in a horse-drawn carriage parked near J. P. Morgan & Company on Wall Street. The power of the blast blew windows out of buildings for blocks. Pieces of glass, steel, and stone flew from the buildings and injured many people. The bomb killed thirty people and wounded about 200. The police thought that this terrorist act might have been committed by **anarchists**. Anti-Soviet feelings in the country made people point the finger at communists. Many different terrorists groups, eager for publicity, claimed to have set off the blast, but no proof of who really planted the bomb was ever found.

# Independence Day Disaster

On July 4, 1925, disaster struck Massachusetts. About 200 members of the Pickwick Club were dancing and celebrating at an Independence Day party on the third floor of the Dreyfus Hotel in Boston. At 3:00 AM, the roof and ceiling of the building caved in. All of the five-story building fell into an open pit that had been dug for construction of a garage. Forty-four people died and many others were injured. It was the city's worst building collapse in history. People were eager to place blame for the accident. Twelve people were **indicted** for manslaughter, including two building officials and the garage contractors. They were all acquitted when the cause of the collapse was shown to be the hotel's rotten concrete pilings.

■ Workers search for survivors in the rubble of the Pickwick Club.

# On the Air

"The radio, or wireless telephony, or what-you-may-call-it isn't even worthy of discussion."

A journalist, after KDKA's first broadcast.

■ The staff at KDKA radio reports the Harding-Cox election results.

On November 2, 1920, a few hundred people tuned in their home receivers to hear the first commercial radio broadcast. Before that day, amateur radio enthusiasts had broadcast over transmitters they had made themselves, and others had received the signals on their own basic receivers. Now, the Pittsburgh radio station KDKA aired its first broadcast. Listeners were rewarded by hearing the results of the presidential election hours before the rest of the country heard them. Westinghouse operated the radio station from the roof of its plant, and the company's name was soon on every American's lips. Radio receivers were immediately in high demand. Westinghouse quickly built stations at its plants across the country, and it manufactured receivers for Americans to tune into these stations. Within a year, hundreds of thousands of people were glued to their radios, listening to play-by-play coverage of the World Series baseball championships. Radio had become a very successful business. By 1922, radio offered companies a way to advertise. The first commercial was aired in 1922 at the cost of $50 for a ten-minute advertisement.

## ROGERS A RIOT

■ Will Rogers started his career as a trick roper and then appeared in more than sixty short and full-length movies. Then he entered politics, but not as a politician. Rogers became a brilliant political satirist who shared his good-natured doubts about the government. Radio gave him an even greater audience. Many Americans thought he really was President Coolidge in 1928 when he delivered his own version of the State of the Union message. This radio joke was heard across the country on forty-five radio stations. Rogers's life was tragically cut short in 1935. He was traveling with the famous aviator Wiley Post when the plane crashed in Alaska.

## And the Oscar Goes To...

The Academy of Motion Picture Arts and Sciences was established in 1927. The organization presented its first awards two years later. The "Awards of Merit" were given to entertainers for work done from 1927 to 1928. The first winners of Academy Awards were Janet Gaynor for her roles in *Seventh Heaven*, *Street Angel*, and *Sunrise*. and Emil Jannings for his performance in *The Last Command* and *The Way of All Flesh*. The top movies of the year were *Wings* for Best Production and *Sunrise* for Best Artistic Film. The gold-plated statue awarded was first called Oscar in 1931. An Academy secretary commented that the statue looked like her Uncle Oscar. The awards ceremony was a five-minute event in 1929. Over the years, the Oscar ceremonies have become extravagant affairs that last several hours.

# The Great Houdini

Audiences were spellbound by Harry Houdini's magical feats. He frequently escaped from shackles, straightjackets, and chained coffins under water. For one of his tricks, Houdini was tied up and locked in a packing case. The case was then tied with steel tape and dropped into the water off New York harbor. Within fifty-nine seconds, Houdini had broken out and come to the surface of the water. Although he explained how many of his tricks were done, it did not make them any less spectacular.

Houdini said that his success was due to his agility, strength, and his way with locks. He assured fans that he was not at all supernatural.

Harry Houdini's daring escape from a Washington, DC, jail was an amazing feat.

He did not believe in mind readers or spiritualists who claimed to talk to the dead. He spent a great deal of time exposing these people as frauds. As final proof, he established a ten-word code with his wife. When he died, any spiritualist who could give her the phrase would win $10,000. Houdini died on Halloween night 1926. As part of his act, he often invited people to punch his stomach as hard as they could—his strong muscles protected him. That day, a man **sucker-punched** Houdini. The entertainer did not have time to flex his muscles, and the blow ruptured his appendix, causing his death. The prize money offered to spiritualists was never claimed.

# Buster Keaton

Buster Keaton had been performing since he was three years old. He made his first movie, *The Butcher Boy*, in 1917 with Fatty Arbuckle. Keaton made more than twelve additional short films over the next three years.

In 1920, Paramount Pictures realized that Keaton was going to be a star and made twenty short movies with him in three years. Many of these productions were very successful.

Keaton developed a character for himself and starred in his first full-length movie in 1920. Over the next several years, he found fame with films such as *The Three Ages* (1923), *Our Hospitality* (1923), *Sherlock, Jr.* (1924), and *Seven Chances*

(1925). When *The General* was released in 1926, Buster Keaton became a megastar. This comedy was thought to be his best work ever. His perfect timing and mastery of **slapstick** comedy delighted audiences. In 1928, MGM Studios bought Keaton's contract. MGM did not give the

■ In *The General*, Buster Keaton tries to track down a stolen locomotive.

comedian control of his work, and it made demands of him that interfered with his creativity. By the mid-thirties, Keaton's reign as the king of comedy was over.

## HOLLYWOOD SPEAKS

■ Until 1927 all movies were silent—without words or music. For years, companies had tried to figure out how to bring sound and film together. The kinks were ironed out, and Bell Labs created a sound-on-disk system. This brought the movie equipment and phonograph records together. Many studios tested the system, called Vitaphone. Warner Brothers decided to apply the technology to the hit play, *The*

*"Wait a minute, wait a minute, you ain't heard nothing yet."*
The first words ever spoken in a movie

*Jazz Singer*. The story was about a man who wanted to be a Broadway singer, but his father wanted him to sing in the synagogue instead. At first, the movie was going to be silent except for the songs, which

included "Toot, Toot, Tootsie, Goodbye," "Mammie," and "Blue Skies." Then the star of the movie, Al Jolson, **ad-libbed** dialogue in two scenes. The rest is history. Audiences were stunned to hear people speaking in a film. Critics raved, and audiences could hardly wait for more talking pictures. *The Jazz Singer* won an Academy Award and earned $3.5 million—an unheard-of amount for the time.

# Mouse Attracts Crowds

In 1928, all eyes in the theater were glued to the screen. They were watching the movements of a mouse. At New York's Colony Theater, a film hero was born. Walt Disney's character Mickey Mouse made his first big-screen appearance in *Steamboat Willie*. Mickey captained a steamboat, made music by squeezing animals to make them moo, bray, or squawk, and rescued his girlfriend, Minnie, from the bad guy. Sound seemed to be the key to Mickey's success. Disney had previously placed him in two silent movies and no one had been interested. Now that sound was used as part of the humor and the story, Mickey was in demand. By the late thirties, Mickey had established himself as one of the most recognizable

■ *Steamboat Willie* remains a classic of U.S. animation.

and most loved characters in the world. Many theaters chose to show Mickey Mouse shorts rather than full-length features. World leaders, such as Franklin Roosevelt, Britain's King George V, and Italy's Benito Mussolini, were all keen Mickey Mouse fans. The final event to show that Mickey Mouse was here to stay was his own entry in *Encyclopaedia Britannica*. Mickey Mouse and the other Disney characters have become a significant part of popular U.S. culture.

WALT DISNEY'S
MICKEY MOUSE
IN
STEAMBOAT WILLIE

## Move Over, Good Girls

After the 1927 movie *The "It" Girl*, Clara Bow became known by the same name. She was a symbol of the **flapper** era— she had bobbed hair, wore short skirts and beaded necklaces, had a pouty mouth, and leaned toward scandal and improper behavior. On the screen, this bubbly actress was one of the biggest stars of silent movies. When movies became talkies, Bow did not do well. Her voice did not go with her image. By 1933, she had retired from movies.

Another Hollywood actress to abandon the "good girl" roles for more daring ones was Mae West. She began as a child actress before working in **vaudeville** and musicals. Her role in Broadway shows, especially *Diamond Lil* (1928), brought her national attention. Her characters were often women who would not conform. They were witty women with questionable morals. Her full-figure, distinctive walk and drawl became her trademarks. The risks she took paid off. By 1935, West was the highest paid woman in the U.S.

■ The popularity of miniature golf quickly spread across the U.S.

# Dancing up a Storm

The Charleston started out as an African-American folk dance. In 1923, it was changed for Broadway's production of *Runnin' Wild*. The lively dance became an instant sensation. Across the country, dancers were slapping their knees, swaying their hips, and swinging their legs to the Charleston. It could be danced alone or with a partner, and it became a social necessity—those who could not do the Charleston were left sitting on the sidelines at social functions. The older generation did not approve. Many thought the way women showed their legs and kicked their feet was indecent. The Charleston was banned in some towns. These bans only made the dance more appealing. Variations of the dance were quickly created, including the Varsity Drag, the Black Bottom, and the Shimmy. Like many fads, the Charleston craze soon died.

## What's New?

The twenties welcomed many new and exciting products and inventions. Here are just a few of the items Americans experienced for the first time:

| |
|---|
| Baby Ruth candy bar (1920) |
| Band-Aid bandages (1921) |
| Skywriting (1922) |
| Warner Brothers Pictures Inc. (1923) |
| Self-winding wristwatch (1924) |
| Dry ice (1925) |
| Miniature golf (1926) |
| Wonder Bread (1927) |
| Bubble gum (1928) |
| Yo-yo (1929) |

## HAVING FUN

■ After World War I, Americans were ready to let loose and have fun. They had more time on their hands. The workweek was reduced from sixty to forty-eight hours. Wages were increased, giving Americans more money to spend. Products and fads reached the population quickly, thanks to mass marketing with ads on the radio and in newspapers. Those who could not afford a product used the new "installment plan." They could buy anything on credit—from a toaster to a new car.

## Slang

**cat's meow**
great, attractive

**big cheese**
a well-to-do man

**beaut**
a cute flapper

**swanky**
high-class

**swell**
great

**necking**
kissing

**hot diggity dog!**
exclamation

# A Six-Letter Word for Fun

■ Gregory Hartswick, a New York reporter, created the crossword puzzle.

Millions of Americans tested their vocabularies with the newest fad—crossword puzzles. The rise in popularity of crossword puzzles led to the rise of one of the biggest publishing houses in the world— Simon & Schuster. The company was formed in 1924 to publish the first collection of crossword puzzles ever printed as a book. These portable puzzles were a great way for people to pass the time while waiting for a bus or sitting on a train on their way to or from work. The books came with a sharpened pencil so that the puzzles could be solved immediately. The puzzle books sold nearly a million copies in one year. While there had been puzzles in newspapers and magazines for years, the public was thrilled to have them in book form. They became one of the biggest trends of the time. A six-letter word for fun in the twenties was "puzzle."

# Sweet Tooth Satisfied

During the twenties, Americans' need for sweets was easily met. Cans and boxes replaced jars, making it less expensive to package and purchase goods. In 1923, Jell-O hit supermarket shelves. This jiggly treat had been around for more than twenty years, but only now was it given the brand name. Ice cream also experienced a revolution. As well as the usual ice cream cones, there were now specialty bars and cones. The Good Humor Bar, the Popsicle, and the Eskimo Pie all made their appearance in the 1920s. The Eskimo Pie sold 1 million

bars a day in its second year on sale. There were also new candies. Americans could pick up Mounds, Milky Way, and Reese's Peanut Butter Cups by 1923. To wash these treats down, companies created bubbly, sweet sodas. The 1920 clear soda, called Howdy, was renamed 7-Up a few years later. For the do-it-yourself Americans, a new drink that was mixed at home hit the market in 1927. By adding sugar and water to the flavored powder, Americans made their own Kool-Aid. This became a popular way to beat the summer heat.

## PLAYING MAH-JONGG

■ It started in California and then took over the country. Mah-jongg was everywhere. This traditional Mandarin game was brought from China after World War I by an American missionary. Americans were intrigued by Asia, so Asian styles or culture were a definite hit. The missionary changed the game slightly and copyrighted it. At the height of the mah-jongg craze in 1923, about 10 million women met regularly at mah-jongg parties and 1.6 million sets were sold.

## Bloody Sunday

The British government had a problem. Most Irish Cathoics wanted "Home Rule"—freedom from British rule. But most Irish Protestants didn't want that because it would give power to the Catholics, who outnumbered them. So, in 1920, Britain divided Ireland, separating the twenty-six mainly Catholic counties in the south from the six mainly Protestant counties in the north. Both north and south were to have their own parliament.

Few people liked this arrangement, and fighting broke out. At its height, the Catholics' Irish Republican Army killed eleven people suspected of helping the British. In retaliation, on November 21, 1920, the police force known as the Black and Tans opened fire on a crowd of people watching a soccer game in a Dublin park. When the massacre was over, twelve spectators were dead and sixty were injured. Anger toward Britain hit an all-time high. In 1922, the British government tried to appease the Catholics by making southern Ireland a self-governing **dominion**. Northern Ireland remained part of the United Kingdom, as the Protestants wanted. This did not please many Catholics, and violence continued.

## Tomb Raiders

For years, archeologists had been searching for the tomb of the Egyptian king, Tutankhamen. The tomb had been buried under another one in 1148 BCE. In 1922, Britain's Howard Carter and his financier, the Earl of Carnarvon, found it. That November, Carter had been exploring the Valley of the Kings in Egypt when he found a staircase buried under some huts. He kept digging. On November 26, he got his first candle-lit glimpse of the 3,000-year-old resting place of Egypt's famous ruler. King Tut, as the boy-king was called, had ruled Egypt from 1333 BCE until he died nine years later. His burial chamber was filled with incredible riches for him to take to the afterlife—he was surrounded by gold, statues, and weapons. The chamber's most amazing treasure, the king himself, was found several months later. The body of the young king was inside three coffins. The one closest to him was made of solid gold. For the first time ever, scientists were able to see how the ancient people buried their kings.

■ Egyptologist Howard Carter examines the solid gold coffin in King Tut's tomb.

# Communist Party in China

I n 1921, when there was a civil war raging in China, small, secret meetings in Shanghai led to the development of the Chinese Communist Party. To avoid the watchful eye of the police, the First Party Congress (as its meetings were dubbed) took place on a boat in the middle of a lake outside the city. Chen Duxiu was one of the founders of the party. He worked to attract new members, and trained them in the Soviet Union, which a few years earlier had

After leading a successful revolution, Mao Tse-tung became the leader of China.

become the first communist nation. Teacher Mao Tse-tung supported the communist movement and became the most important Chinese communist leader of the century. He organized strikes, fought against war lords, and helped build the Red Army. Other influential people, including Deng Xiaoping and Zhou Enlai, were involved in the Communist Party at the start and became important world players.

## TALKING TURKEY

Mustafa Kemal was a Turkish commander in World War I and a hero in the Ottoman Empire. After the war, the empire began to crumble. Rather than fighting to rebuild it, Kemal called for the systems of the old empire to be destroyed completely. With army backing, he established a provisional government in Ankara to revolt against the sultan's government in Constantinople.

The Chamber of Deputies in Constantinople supported the independence plan in 1920. The British immediately moved in with troops and disbanded the chamber. Kemal was not discouraged. He held elections to fill the new Grand National Assembly. The sultan's army stopped Kemal's forces in some areas, and reclaimed territory that had been lost long ago to other countries. They took back land from Armenia, Georgia, and France. The British would not back down. A year-long war developed between the two, with Greece supporting the British efforts. After a terrible loss in Anatolia, Greece pulled out of the conflict. In 1923, the Allies signed the Treaty of Lausanne. A few months later, the Turkish Republic was formed with Kemal as its president. He gave women the vote, separated the church from the government, and tried to modernize the country. He later changed his name to Ataturk. He is honored as the founder of modern Turkey.

# Soviet Successor

In 1924, the father of Soviet Communism, Vladimir Lenin, was dying. His advisors all wanted to succeed him as leader. When Lenin died of a stroke, the party was split. On one side was Joseph Stalin, Lev Kamenev, and Grigory Zinoviev. On the other was Leon Trotsky, who many thought was the true successor. Stalin delivered speeches about his lost leader and promised to carry on the great man's work. Trotsky, on the other hand, was receiving medical treatment miles away.

Stalin gained the support of Soviets and pushed Trotsky out of the picture. In 1925, he removed Trotsky as commissar of war. Then Stalin kicked Kamenev and Zinoviev out of the politburo, the governing body of

the party. Bitter, they joined Trotsky to bring Stalin down. The new leader easily discredited the pact, passing it off as a group of disgruntled, unpatriotic men. Trotsky was **exiled** in 1929. Kamenev and Zinoviev were allowed to stay in the Soviet Union but they could not be

■ Vladimir Lenin (left) and Joseph Stalin sit together shortly before Lenin's death.

part of the government. In 1936, they were both tried and executed for treason. Stalin finally got what he wanted—complete control over the Soviet Union.

## TAKING BACK IRAN

■ Britain, Germany, and the Soviet Union had all fought for control of Persia, which is present-day Iran. In 1919, Britain pulled out of the area. The result was upheaval. Reza Khan, an army officer, stepped in to take over power. In 1925, he deposed the reigning shah and proclaimed himself shah. Now called Shah Reza, he promised to bring the country into the twentieth century. He updated

Islamic divorce laws so that women had some control over their lives. He said that women no longer had to wear veils to cover their faces. European dress was acceptable for both men and women. Shah Reza built the first railroad in Iran and worked to improve education and sanitation in the country. He also boosted the economy. He worked out better oil agreements, gaining more control of this valuable resource. Despite

the advances and improvements, Shah Reza's methods were harsh. He gave to Iran, but he also took much for himself, seizing large plots of land for personal use. He backed Germany during World War II. When Britain and the Soviet Union wanted a clear path to the Russian **front**, they moved into Iran and forced the shah to step down.

## Gandhi Fasts for Peace

Mohandas Gandhi, called Mahatma, meaning "Great Soul," had for years been trying to gain independence from Britain for India. To aid this cause, he encouraged his followers to disobey the British, but to do so peacefully, without violence. In 1922, Gandhi called off his civil disobedience campaign because a riot in a small village had led to the deaths of British civil servants. When Gandhi halted his campaign, many Indians stopped supporting him. The British government took this opportunity to put him on trial and jail him for **inciting** people to rebel against authority. He spent two years in prison and was released in 1924. Meanwhile, the leaders of the independence movement had stopped following Gandhi's policy of peaceful resistance. To make matters worse, the country experiencing religious intolerance, with Indian Hindus fighting against Indian Muslims. On his release, Gandhi quickly regained political influence. He embarked on a twenty-one-day fast for unity and tolerance as he had done many times before when leading non-violent protests. Gandhi again became the people's central figure in the fight for independence.

## Mussolini's Rise

After World War I, Italian politicians promised better times. They could not deliver. The unemployment numbers skyrocketed. Democracy was not working, and people were desperate for change. The **fascist** party leader, Benito Mussolini, stepped in to provide it. On October 28, 1922, 40,000 fascist followers marched on Rome. They were not well organized or equipped. The army could easily have quashed the rebellion. King Vittorio Emmanuel III panicked. Instead of sending in the military, he offered Mussolini partial control over a new cabinet. Mussolini refused. The king called him the next day and asked him to create a new government. Mussolini accepted and took over the government.

By 1926, many people were unhappy with Mussolini. Between April and October, there were four attempts to assassinate him. In response, he took control of the media. He passed laws allowing him to rule without consulting the legislature. He replaced elected officials with his supporters. Parliament was dissolved and replaced by a body of appointed fascists. Mussolini's special police force was feared—it judged political crimes and carried out punishment quickly, secretly, and without appeals. Some Italians supported Mussolini, saying his was the only way to avoid chaos. Others were angry at the repression in Italy. Now, anyone who opposed Mussolini had to stay quiet or risk death. Mussolini finally had complete control over Italy.

■ Fascist dictator Benito Mussolini stands above the crowd during a rally.

# Women at the Ballot Boxes

During and after World War I, women were given the right to vote in several countries—in the Soviet Union in 1917, in Canada and Britain in 1918, and in Austria, Poland, Germany, and Czechoslovakia in 1919. The U.S. followed suit in 1920. While other countries limited these rights, the U.S. was the first country to give every female citizen over twenty-one years of age the same right to vote as male citizens. The nineteenth amendment, which gave women this right, had been a long time coming. For about eighty years, women had been fighting for equal voting rights. Not everyone supported this change. Some people argued that the right to vote would make women less feminine and destroy the family unit. The nineteenth amendment had been on the table since 1918. It had been stalled because some southern legislators were afraid of what would happen if both women and African Americans were allowed to vote. The law was rejected twice before being passed by two-thirds of the states. Women across the country, regardless of race or social standing, could finally cast their ballots and influence how their country was run.

## America Goes Dry

Many people believed that alcohol created a disorderly society of people without morals. Drunkenness was blamed for family breakdown, crime, poverty, and violence. The government set out to put people on the right path. As of January 16, 1920, Americans could no longer legally buy or sell alcohol. The eighteenth amendment banned "intoxicating liquors." The law was called Prohibition. Prohibition was difficult to enforce. Police units could raid only so many **bootleggers** or **speakeasies**.

Many people saw the law as an invasion of their private lives. Some people argued that the emphasis on alcohol and the laws to ban it caused people to drink more rather than less. Others saw Prohibition as an opportunity to make money. Bootleggers, including some gangsters, distilled and provided alcohol to those willing to pay for it. Nightclubs selling liquor popped up one night and relocated the next to avoid being found by the police. As the twenties roared on, many Americans resented the government for trampling on their individual freedoms. They formed organizations to put an end to Prohibition. When the Great Depression hit in the thirties, a new argument for **repealing** the law arose—that the ban on the alcohol industry was taking away badly needed jobs and government revenue. In 1933, the twenty-first amendment repealed Prohibition.

New York State Troopers unload cases of bootlegged alcohol confiscated during the prohibition era.

# Silent Cal

President Warren Harding and Vice President Calvin Coolidge took office in 1921. People did not expect much from Coolidge—he oversaw the Senate, attended Cabinet meetings, and accompanied the president to ceremonies and other functions. He was nicknamed "Silent Cal," but he was not silent for long. Coolidge began to express his opinions in speeches and newspaper articles.

By 1923, the administration was in trouble. The 1922 business slump had not picked up. In the election, the Republicans lost the majority rule in both houses of Congress. Some Republican senators were angry about agricultural issues and threatened to side with the Democrats. The final straw was the Teapot Dome Scandal. When Harding died in

August 1923, Calvin Coolidge stepped in as president to regain the public's trust.

■ President Warren G. Harding and First Lady Florence Harding celebrate victory.

## SCANDAL IN WASHINGTON

■ When Warren Harding was elected president, his secretary of the interior, Albert Bacon Fall, convinced the president to transfer operation of two naval oil reserves to the Department of the Interior. One was in Elk Hills, California, and the other was in Teapot Dome, Wyoming. Fall then sold drilling rights and secretly leased the reserves to private companies in 1922, making an enormous personal profit. He was bribed with $400,000 and government bonds to complete the deals. The Senate was suspicious of Fall. He had entered office broke and was now buying land and cattle for his ranch.

An investigation was launched in 1923 to delve into the Teapot Dome Scandal. This phrase came to symbolize the corruption in Harding's administration. While Harding was thought to be completely ignorant of what had happened, those close to him were not given the same consideration. As the details of the corruption came to light, two of Harding's advisors—Jess Smith of the Justice Department and Charles Cramer of Veterans Affairs—committed suicide. The President was very upset. He came down with a mysterious illness and died on August 2, 1923. While food poisoning and exhaustion were blamed, some thought the president was a victim of foul play. Some years later, Fall was sent to prison for his part in the scandal.

## Campaigning for President

When Calvin Coolidge took over the presidency, he set out to repair the damage done to the government by the various scandals. He demanded the resignation of Secretary of the Navy, Edwin Denby, for his role in the Teapot Dome Scandal. He also dismissed the attorney general, Harry Daugherty, who had been selling alcohol illegally.

Then he turned his attention to the economy. By the time of the 1924 presidential election, the finances of the country had improved and people thanked Coolidge for boosting the economy. He ran for the presidency with the slogan "Keep Cool With Coolidge." This referred to the tension in the Democratic party. Delegates were split on who they wanted representing them.

John Davis won the Democratic nomination, but many working-class Americans did not support him—they saw him as being money-centered. Workers who had traditionally voted Democrat changed their vote to Republican. Coolidge easily won the election and was sworn in as the thirtieth president on March 4, 1925.

## Coolidge at the Helm

In 1925, Congress enjoyed a Republican majority. That did not mean that it always supported the president. The financial boom did not trickle down to struggling farmers and ranchers, and Republican representatives of the agricultural areas began to join forces with like-minded Democrats. The McNary-Haugen Farm Relief Bill was the result. This proposal asked the government to buy extra crops and sell them overseas so that U.S. agricultural prices would go up. Coolidge refused. He said that the government should not fix prices. The bill was quashed in 1927 and again in 1928. The representatives also fought Coolidge's tax reforms, especially breaks for high-income earners. The tax bills had to go through many changes before being passed. At the same time, Coolidge refused bills that would give extra money to World War I veterans and to a government-operated hydroelectric plant in Alabama. Coolidge supported private enterprise and he did not want the government to interfere.

■ President Calvin and Mrs. Coolidge leave the White House.

His attitude won him support in some areas and fierce opposition in others.

# Hoover Pulls Out Stops

President Coolidge decided not to compete in the 1928 presidential race, and Herbert Hoover gained the Republican nomination. Hoover had served as the secretary of commerce under Coolidge, and his name was associated with the financial good times the country enjoyed. During the election campaign, he used technology whenever he could. He broadcast speeches over the radio and recorded his messages on film. His opponent, Democrat Al Smith, could not compete. Once all the ballots were counted, Hoover was declared a runaway winner. He gained

444 electoral votes to Smith's 87, and he received 21,437,277 popular votes, whereas Smith received only 15,007,698. Hoover claimed every Northern state except Massachusetts and Rhode Island, and he stole the traditionally Democratic South by winning Virginia, North Carolina, Florida, Tennessee, and Texas. President Hoover had won by one of the biggest margins in U.S. electoral history.

■ President Herbert Hoover takes off his hat in recognition of the crowds surrounding his car in a parade in San Francisco, California.

## SCOPES TRIAL

■ In 1925, the Tennessee government passed the Butler Act, making it illegal to teach the evolutionary theory in schools. Anyone teaching anything to deny the Bible's story of divine creation was subject to fines of up to $500. Twenty-four-year-old John Scopes graduated from the University of Kentucky and began teaching science in Rhea County in Dayton. He taught evolution, just as he had learned in Kentucky. He was charged with violating the Butler Act. The trial that followed was soon dubbed the Monkey Trial because people associated evolution with descent from monkeys. Scopes was convicted and fined $100. The Supreme Court later reversed the verdict. The case attracted national attention, and a 1960 movie, *Inherit the Wind*, was based on it. The Butler Act remained law until 1967.

## Farm Relief

Unlike his predecessor, President Hoover was sympathetic toward the farmers and ranchers. He called a special session of Congress in April 1929 to try to help. He enacted the Agricultural Marketing Act. This was the first time a large government system was put in place to help

farmers during peacetime. Hoover also established the Federal Farm Board. The eight members of the board doled out loans to marketing cooperatives. The board could also create corporations to buy extra crops and products so that prices could rise. Within six months, the Great Depression began to sweep the country. The price of farm products fell to an all-time

low. Until 1931, Hoover's initiatives kept wheat and cotton prices slightly above world levels. By the following year, government money for the project was gone. The Farm Board could not buy products to help stabilize the prices. The price of agricultural products continued to drop throughout the Great Depression.

# The Greatness of Gatsby

■ F. Scott Fitzgerald wrote several literary masterpieces.

SUN RISES
FOR HEMINGWAY

■ Ernest Hemingway's 1926 novel *The Sun Also Rises* was an instant hit. It spoke for the "lost generation," a term Hemingway borrowed from writer Gertrude Stein to describe Americans in their twenties and early thirties. They were left to wade through the social changes and chaos left after World War I. University students immediately adopted Hemingway's blunt and tired way of speaking. His influence could be seen in manuscripts of countless aspiring writers. They tried to recreate Hemingway's unique style. The attention and success of the novel launched Hemingway into the realm of the literary superstar. *The Sun Also Rises* is about a group of American and British artists and writers living in France. The unhappy characters look unsuccessfully for fulfillment in cafés and nightclubs. Hemingway was also successful with *A Farewell to Arms* (1929), a love story of an American soldier in the ambulance service and a British nurse, set in wartime Italy. For the next several decades, Hemingway wrote more thought-provoking novels, as well as short stories. He died in 1961 at the age of 61.

By the time F. Scott Fitzgerald was 29 years old, he had written a play and four books, including his hit first novel, *This Side of Paradise* (1920). He was also praised for *The Beautiful and Damned* (1922), a story of wealth and the destruction it can bring. Then, in 1925, Fitzgerald published *The Great Gatsby*. The novel again followed the glamorous lives of wealthy Americans in the Jazz Age. The characters in the novel float from party to party and from romance to romance. The book's namesake, Jay Gatsby, builds his wealth through bootlegging, all to win the love of a married socialite named Daisy. *The Great Gatsby* is narrated by Nick Carraway. He exposes the wealthy for what they are and criticizes them for confusing the American Dream with the need for power and money. In the end, the characters are destroyed by themselves and their vices. Many critics feel that *The Great Gatsby* was Fitzgerald's best work. It is one of the twentieth century's great masterpieces of fiction and is on the reading list of most American literature courses in universities and high schools.

# W❂RLD FOCUS

## AGATHA ADDS A HERO

*Agatha Christie wrote her first mystery novel after her sister claimed she had never read a mystery in which she did not know right away "whodunit."*

*Christie's* Mysterious Affair at Styles *introduced one of the most famous crime-solvers in fiction—Hercule Poirot. The novel was sent to several publishers before The Bodley Head accepted it. Published in 1920, it was followed by thirty-six other very popular mystery novels, all featuring Poirot. Then, in 1930, Christie introduced an unlikely mystery detective—Miss Jane Marple, an elderly woman who had a knack for cracking cases. Over the next fifty years, Poirot and Marple appeared in more than eighty novels, including* The Murder of Roger Ackroyd

■ Agatha Christie at work in her home in Devon, England.

*(1926) and* Murder on the Orient Express *(1934). Christie's work has inspired movies, television series, and theater productions. Her play* The Mousetrap *has been performed in London, England, non-stop since 1952.*

# The Innocence of Edith Wharton

Edith Wharton's writing often dealt with the **ethics** and manners of upper-class characters. Her 1920 novel *The Age of Innocence* looked at New York high society and the ethical problems its people had. The main character, Newland Archer, is engaged to one woman and in love with her European cousin. Wharton's novel compared the morality, or perceived lack of morality, of Europeans with the moral values of Americans. The novel brought Wharton great success. She won the 1921 Pulitzer Prize for the novel, becoming the first woman to earn the honor. In 1923, she was awarded an honorary degree from Yale University. She was again the first woman to be given such a distinction. Wharton's two best-known works, *The Age of Innocence* and *Ethan Frome* (1911), were made into movies in 1993. This brought renewed attention to Wharton's writings. *Edith Wharton: The Uncollected Critical Writings* was published in 1996, nearly sixty years after her death.

## Time for a Change

Two Yale graduates decided it was their duty to inform Americans. Henry Luce and Briton Hadden launched their weekly news magazine, *Time*, in 1923. *Time* hit newsstands on March 3 and cost readers fifteen cents. The magazine gave readers a recap of the week's news taken from scores of daily newspapers.

Hadden died of a strep infection in 1929, but Luce continued to further the success of the magazine. Within ten years, Time Inc. established its own news-gathering system and became a highly successful publication. Today it is one of the most popular magazines in the country.

## Aviator Crosses the Atlantic

Other people had flown across the Atlantic, but Charles Lindbergh was the first to do it alone. A French hotel owner in New York was offering a $25,000 prize to anyone who flew nonstop from New York to France, and Lindbergh decided to give it a try. On May 20, 1927, he flew out of Long Island, New York, at 7:54 AM. He landed at Le Bourget airport in Paris thirty-three and a half hours later.

He had not slept the night before the flight, so he had to fight to stay awake during the 3,614-mile journey. Fog, storms, and instability due to the light weight of the plane added to his troubles. But he touched down safely. About 100,000 cheering fans were there to greet him. Many of them wanted a souvenir of the incredible journey, and the *Spirit*

> "I saw a fleet of fishing boats...I flew down almost touching the craft and yelled at them, asking if I was on the right road to Ireland...An hour later I saw land."
>
> Charles Lindburgh, after his solo flight

Charles Lindbergh stands in front of his plane, *Spirit of St. Louis.*

*of St. Louis* plane was nearly torn apart. In June, when he returned to the U.S., 4 million people were gathered to welcome him. Lindbergh used his fame to promote commercial overseas air travel. By 1935, Pan Am began offering passengers flights across the Pacific Ocean. Lindbergh's dream was a reality.

## ICY INVENTION

Americans were used to having the "iceman" track mud through their kitchens as he delivered blocks of ice for their iceboxes. Experiments with mechanical refrigeration started in the early 1900s. Business people, including fur-vault owners and dairy operators, were looking for a better way to keep their products cool. This led to advances in home refrigeration, too. In 1923, Frigidaire, a division of the huge company General Motors, revolutionized U.S. kitchens. Its new machine had a separate cabinet for the icebox, complete with machinery to keep it cool. The refrigerator was small, neat, and convenient. Soon, nearly every family scrambled to buy a Frigidaire. By 1944, about 85 percent of American families owned one. This invention put an end to the muddy footprints and to iceboxes forever.

## Hollywood in Technicolor

In 1922, black and white movies were given a splash of color. Herbert T. Kalmus and Daniel F. Comstock had begun to tackle the challenge of colorizing film in 1915 with their company, Technicolor Motion Picture Company. They soon thought of using a camera that had two strips of film—one for green and the other for red—and a **prism** to separate the light into the primary colors. The strips were brought together when the film was developed and printed. This was exciting because no special projectors or filters were needed to achieve color. The first movie made using the Technicolor process was the 1922 remake of *Madama Butterfly* called *Toll of the Sea*. The film met great reviews, but the new color did not catch on. It was too expensive for producers to use. Technicolor was often used to bring color to special sequences or scenes in otherwise black and white films until around 1930. Three-color Technicolor was developed and first used by Walt Disney in his animated films. The full-length movie *Becky Sharp* (1935) was the first film to use the three-color process.

## WORLD FOCUS

*One of the most deadly diseases in the world in the twenties was tuberculosis. In 1921, after fifteen years of experimenting, a vaccine was found to increase children's resistance to the horrible disease. French scientists Albert Léon Calmette and Camille Guérin created the vaccine from a weakened strain of live tuberculosis bacteria. They injected schoolchildren with this strain to stop the spread of this incurable disease. Most European countries accepted the vaccine, but the treatment was not offered in the U.S. and also in Europe. American scientists were nervous about the vaccine—in Germany in 1930, 73 of the 249 infants vaccinated died within a year of being injected. The U.S. and British authorities accepted the vaccine in 1940. By the time of Guérin's death in 1961, 200 million people worldwide had taken advantage of the tuberculosis vaccine.*

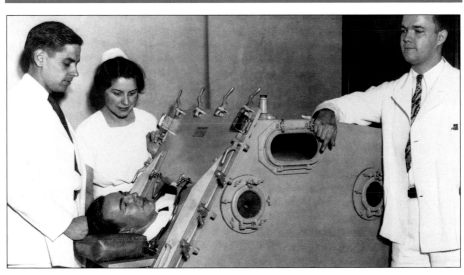

■ Staff monitor a patient in an iron lung at the Sister Kenny Institute.

## Iron Lung Helps Americans Breathe

Poliomyelitis, or polio, was a terrible disease that struck the central nervous system. Young children were at risk of contracting this disease. Before 1927, doctors could do little for patients as polio paralyzed their lungs. The patients slowly suffocated. In 1927, Harvard physician Philip Drinker created a machine that helped people breathe. This artificial breather was nicknamed "the iron lung." It moved air in and out of a chamber with the help of a vacuum pump. Patients would lie within the tank-like chamber, and the movement of the air forced the lungs to inflate. Patients were kept alive in these iron lungs until they recovered from polio. This invention saved the lives of many polio victims until a vaccine in the fifties essentially wiped out the disease in North America.

■ Babe Ruth practices his batting technique.

# The Babe

George Ruth, better known as Babe, remains one of the most popular athletes in history. He was known throughout the world for more than his talent on the baseball field. His charisma attracted many fans. Japan even declared a "Babu Rusu Day" to honor the New York Yankee outfielder. He had many nicknames, including "Bambino," which is Italian for "babe," and the "Sultan of Swat" for his powerful bat. In 1920, the Yankees offered Ruth the amazing sum of $125,000 to play for the team. The following year, he smashed fifty-nine home runs over the fence. This made him even more popular in New York. The new stadium was officially named Yankee Stadium, but it was commonly called "The House that Ruth Built." Ruth won ten home run titles and helped the Yankees win four World Series championships.

During the playoffs in 1926, Ruth heard about a young fan in hospital. He wrote the boy a telegram, promising to hit a home run for him that day. He did better than that. He hit three.

Ruth held many Major League records. In 1927, he hit sixty regular-season home runs—a record that would last until Roger Maris hit sixty-one in 1961. Ruth's career home run record of 714 stood until 1974, when Hank Aaron broke it. In his twenty-two years as a professional baseball player, Babe Ruth played 2,503 games, had a batting average of .342, drove in 2,213 runs, and was walked 2,056 times. He is often thought of as the best player to ever walk on the diamond.

## TILDEN ALL ACES

■ "Big Bill" Tilden lobbed and aced his way into the record books in 1920. He was the best and most powerful tennis player of the time. In 1920, Tilden won the U.S. National Singles Championship. He defended that title five years running. For the entire decade, Tilden was part of the U.S. Davis Cup team. He contributed to seven championships in a row, from 1920 to 1926. In 1920, he became the first U.S. player to win Britain's Wimbledon tennis championships. He won it again in 1921 and 1930. By 1929, Tilden had reclaimed the U.S. singles championship and also taken the singles titles in Switzerland and the Netherlands. Tilden won many doubles titles as well, including those in 1921, 1922, and 1927. He took the mixed doubles championships four times, including the 1922 and 1923 contests. By the time Tilden turned professional in 1931, he had a record sixteen U.S. championships under his belt. Bill Tilden completely dominated tennis throughout the twenties and made it more than a country-club event. It was always an exciting spectacle when "Big Bill" was on the court.

# Caddy Shows His Stuff

Gene Sarazen started playing golf as a young boy. As well, he used to **caddy** for other golfers so he could earn money and still be around the game. In 1922, when he was twenty-one, he won the U.S. Open and the U.S. Professional Golfers Association (USPGA) championships. He was the first golfer to win both titles in the same year. He defended his USPGA title in 1923. From 1927 to 1937, he was also a member of the Ryder Cup teams.

Sarazen competed in exhibitions for the rest of the decade, but he did not win another major tournament until 1932. Then he won the U.S. Open and the British Open. In 1935, he won the Masters tournament. This made him the first golfer to have won the four major tournaments of the time— the British Open, the Masters, the U.S. Open, and the USPGA. At the Masters, he made one of the best-known shots in the history of the game—he got an albatross (which is three strokes under par) on the fifteenth hole, tying him for the lead. Famed as one of the greatest golfers of the 1920s and 1930s, Sarazen was elected to the Professional Golf Association Hall of Fame in 1941.

## The Galloping Ghost

For nearly twenty years, Harold "Red" Grange ruled the football field. He enrolled at the University of Illinois to play baseball and basketball. His fraternity brothers convinced him to go out for football instead. Number seventy-seven made the coaches notice him— to introduce himself, he returned a punt and scored a 65-yard touchdown. From then on, Grange was a local celebrity. Previously, college football had been a campus interest. Now it was a city-wide sensation followed by millions of people. In his first year, Grange was named an All-American. He was given that honor twice more before graduating.

The Galloping Ghost once scored five touchdowns in twelve minutes.

In 1924, the talented halfback scored five touchdowns the first five times he received the ball. This prompted sportswriter Grantland Rice to dub him the "Galloping Ghost." With Grange's help, the University of Illinois dethroned the college kings of the gridiron.

Its victories over the University of Michigan in 1924 and the University of Philadelphia in 1925 went down in the history books. During his time at the university, Grange scored thirty-one touchdowns in twenty games. After graduating, he signed football's first big professional contract with the Chicago Bears. He was offered $100,000 and a share of the admission profits. Most other footballers were making $25 to $100 per game. Grange retired from the sport in 1934 and was inducted into the Pro Football Hall of Fame in 1963.

# NHL Adds Americans

In 1924, the Boston Bruins became the first U.S. team to join the National Hockey League. Other American teams soon followed. In their first game, the Bruins beat the Montreal Maroons 2–1. But this victory was not a sign of things to come. The Bruins lost the next eleven games. Despite the goal-scoring power of Jimmy Herberts, the team finished the season in last place. The following season, the Bruins improved their record, but not by much. They ended up fourth. Their third year in the league, the Bruins battled their way to the Stanley Cup playoffs, but lost to the Ottawa Senators. Big names, including Eddie Shore, Harry Oliver, and Frank Frederickson, drew fans to the arena and put points to the scoreboard. In the 1927–28 season, the Bruins won the Prince of Wales Trophy for their first-place finish in the American Division, but they were knocked out of the playoffs by the New York Rangers. In the 1928–29 season, all the Bruins' hard work was realized. The first championship final between U.S. teams resulted in a Bruins victory. They won their first Stanley Cup on March 29, 1929.

## The Long Count

On September 22, 1927, about 150,000 excited boxing fans filled Chicago's Soldier Field. This was a record showing for a sporting event. The draw: the heavyweight championship match between champ Gene Tunney and challenger Jack Dempsey. Tunney had taken the title from Dempsey the year before and it was advertised as the grudge match— Dempsey wanted his heavyweight belt back.

It did not take long for Dempsey to take control. He sent Tunney to the canvas with blow after blow, but he did not return to his corner after knocking Tunney down, as the rules stated he must. The referee would not start the count until Dempsey was in his corner. It took Tunney until the count of nine (with ten being a knockout) to get to his feet again. Tunney came back to win the match. Fans and sports journalists claimed that Tunney had an unfair chance to recover from the attack because the count did not start until five seconds after Tunney had been

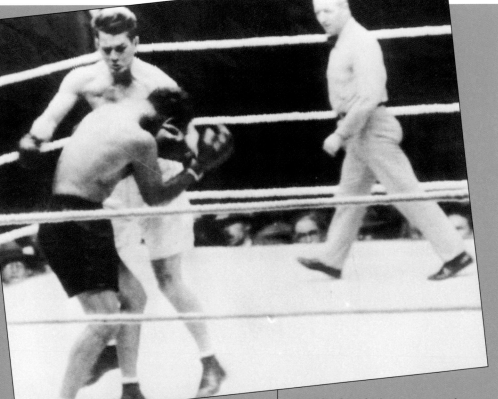

■ The battle between Jack Dempsey and Gene Tunney kept fans on the edge of their seats.

knocked down. The match became one of boxing's most **controversial** and was dubbed the "Battle of the Long Count." After this tough loss, Dempsey retired from boxing. Tunney retired in 1928 with an undefeated record as a heavyweight.

# Flexing Muscles

Charles Atlas was born Angelo Siciliano. As a child, he was small and timid. The 97-pound weakling was tired of being bullied, so he trained as hard as he could to build muscle. He used the statues of Hercules he saw in the Brooklyn Museum as his inspiration. After years of hard work and training, Atlas was successful. In 1922, *Physical Culture* magazine named the 28-year-old the "World's Most Perfectly Developed Man." For two years, the magazine had sponsored a bodybuilding competition, and Atlas had won both times. The contest was stopped because the magazine figured that Atlas would win every time. He had built his perfect body using what he called "dynamic tension," or isometrics. This is a technique that tenses one muscle group in opposition to another group or against immovable objects. By 1927, Atlas's enormous build was enormously profitable. He offered help to others who wanted to bulk up. His mail-order business earned the bodybuilder $1,000 each day.

■ **Charles Atlas flexes his muscles.**

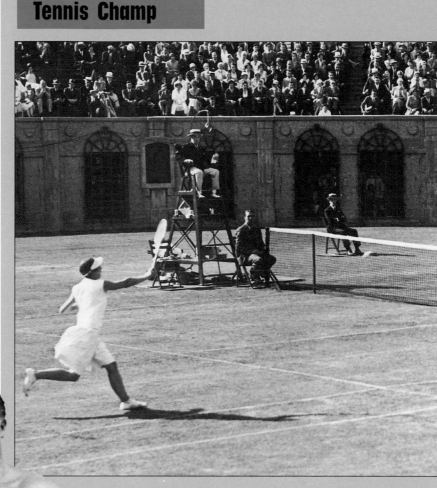

## Tennis Champ

■ In 1926, Helen Wills won the first of eight Wimbledon titles.

Helen Wills was one of the best female tennis players in the history of the game. During her long career, she won nineteen singles titles at tournaments around the world. In 1922, at the age of sixteen, Wills surprised the tennis community by making it to the U.S. championship finals. She played without emotion, earning her the nickname "Little Miss Poker Face." Her powerful forehand made her virtually unbeatable during the 1920s. In 1924, Wills won gold medals in singles and doubles competitions at the Olympic Games in Paris, France. She took home the U.S. women's singles championship seven times. In Britain, she dominated the Wimbledon championships, taking home the top prize in 1927, 1928, 1929, 1930, 1932, 1935, and 1938. Her success continued in France, where she won the singles titles in 1928, 1929, 1930, and 1932. She retired in 1938. She was inducted into the U.S. Lawn Tennis Hall of Fame in 1959.

## The Red Scare

Following the Russian Revolution of 1917, fear of communism swept the nation. Russians living in the U.S. were targeted. The Union of Russian Workers was raided, and many members were arrested and beaten. Of the 250 members, there were grounds to deport only thirty-nine. Attorney General A. Mitchell Palmer teamed up with the Labor Department and successfully deported 249 Russians. Most of these people had done nothing wrong and were not even communists. By 1920, raids were common across the country. About 6,000 people were arrested, many of whom were non-communist American citizens. Few Americans spoke out against the unfair treatment of these people. Still, Palmer feared a revolution, and he warned Americans about these so-called Red Plots. Eventually, people became bored with his ranting. The Red Scare was over, but the effects of it did not go away. Palmer's orders had violated the rights of people. Hundreds of innocent people had been **deported**. Many states, caught up in the hysteria, passed harsh laws against uprisings. This led to immigration restrictions and racial intolerance throughout the decade and beyond.

SIBERIE

PAIX ET LIBERTE

■ In the 1920s, society viewed communists as being war-hungry and evil.

## Renaissance in Harlem

Harlem, in New York City, had been a fashionable neighborhood. By the twenties, it was one of the poorest urban areas in the continent. After World War I, the neighborhood was the site of the African-American artistic movement called the Harlem Renaissance. Clubs and cabarets, including the Cotton Club, sprang up in the area. People flocked to Harlem to hear the latest and greatest jazz musicians perform their favorite songs.

The area also produced many talented authors, who wrote about the African-American experience. Countee Cullen, James Weldon Johnson, Zora Neale Hurston, and Claude McKay were among these writers. The style of these books varied, but they touched on many of the same ideas. McKay's *Home to Harlem* told the story of an African-American soldier home from World War I. Rudolph Fisher's *Walls of Jericho* was unconventional—it explored the class structure in Harlem. Poet Langston Hughes used blues and jazz and strong language to talk about the experiences of African Americans. His work appeared in newspapers, magazines, and anthologies. The Harlem Renaissance, like most things in the twenties, ended when the market crashed in 1929, but the movement laid the groundwork for future African-American artists and writers.

## WOMEN'S MOVEMENT

■ The decade began with women being given the right to vote. That was not enough for many twenties women. They wanted equality in other areas as well. They demanded easier and fairer divorces. They also looked for equal access to jobs and income. They wanted to be able to choose to live on their own in their own apartments, thanks to a steady and fair paycheck. Flappers were seen as modern women. They dressed as they wished, and did not conform to society's idea of "womanhood." Women were standing up for themselves, much to the dismay of many people, including their own mothers. The push toward equality continued for decades.

■ After fighting to win the right to vote, women across the country fought to keep it.

# Race Relations

On July 4, 1923, most Americans joined together in a celebration of the nation's birthday. Some took part in a more sinister event. In Indiana, thousands of men, women, and children, dressed in white robes and pointed hoods, gathered at a Ku Klux Klan (KKK) rally. It was the largest KKK rally ever held in a northern state. Estimates of the number who attended range from 10,000 to 200,000. The Klan was founded after the Civil War to protect the rights of white Americans by terrorizing African Americans. The KKK had been inactive for fifty years, but it resurfaced in the twenties. Speeches, picnics, parades, and cross burnings marked the organization's return. By 1925, the KKK had 4 million members. They targeted not only African Americans but also Jewish Americans, Catholics, immigrants, and alcohol bootleggers. The 1925 trial and conviction of Indiana's Klan chief for second-degree murder made many Americans rethink their **affiliation** with the KKK. By 1930, membership had dropped to around 100,000, made up mostly of Americans in the South.

# Good Times

**Thanks to the booming economy, shopping districts such as this one in Chicago were always crowded.**

President Coolidge's policies had helped the economy. People across the country were working, except in a few industries, such as coal and textiles. By 1923, industrial workers were earning twice what they had in 1914. Their wages continued to climb until 1928. By then, wages across the board were about one-third higher than they had been in 1923. This was partly because cheap energy kept manufacturing and shipping costs low. As well, employers thought that offering higher wages would prevent their workers from wanting to join labor unions. Since Americans were earning decent wages, they spent more money and bought more goods. This helped the manufacturers and store keepers. The price of food fell, as did goods manufactured in industries that were mechanized. As a result, earnings could buy even more goods than before. Americans continued to make and spend money until the stock market crash in 1929.

## ROARING TWENTIES

The twenties really began to roar in 1923. The recession experienced after World War I was over. Stock market values hit the roof. The gross national product was up 14 percent from 1922, and only 2.4 percent of the population was unemployed. Americans were encouraged to spend their new-found wealth on themselves. Mass-produced cars, cosmetics, and clothing were trumpeted as must-haves. After the horrors of war, Americans wanted to have fun, and they spent their money on products that helped them achieve that goal. Now that they had shorter workweeks, there was more time to spend on leisure activities with family and friends. People across the country were eager to live life to the fullest.

## Boom Time

Not since the Wild West of the 1800s had there been such a land boom. Tens of thousands of people rushed to Florida to get in on the action. They were eager to buy pieces of the state that had been advertised as paradise. The warm climate and the idea of an American Riviera like the one in France attracted investors by the hundred. Many buyers agreed to purchase land without seeing it first. They often discovered too late that they were the new owners of swampland. The land boom in Florida was at its height in 1925. A devastating hurricane in 1926 brought it to an abrupt end, destroying developments and the railroad to Key West.

## Crash Destroys Thousands

It seemed as though the good times and good fortune of the twenties would never end. But they did. The economic boom fizzled quickly on October 24, 1929 with the New York Stock Exchange crash. Thousands of Americans lost everything they owned. By the end of the day, the pressure and stress pushed eleven financiers to commit suicide. The day became known as Black Thursday.

Although there were some warning signs, the financial bust came as a surprise to most Americans. Since 1925, the stock prices had more than doubled and the Dow Jones, which measured the value of major stocks, had reached record highs. At the same time, the world economy was slowing and stocks were very overpriced. Many investors listened to these warnings and cashed in their shares. As more people pulled out of the market, the stock prices dropped. On October 19, Americans across the country scrambled to dump their stocks. For five days, investors sold and prices plummeted. Then the bottom fell out of the stock market, and panic swept the country.

Many companies went out of business. Those who survived cut back on production and employees. Millions of people were out of work. Wages and prices fell, and people bought only essential goods. Banks demanded loan and mortgage paybacks. Thousands of people were ruined. The government thought the system would correct itself, so it did little to help. By 1933, unemployment skyrocketed, people were hungry, and there was no end in sight. The Great Depression lasted until the late 1930s.

■ Crowds, cars, and mounted policemen gather on a New York street shortly after the stock market crash.

# Mellon Axes Taxes

Treasury secretary Andrew W. Mellon, one of the country's richest men, believed that low taxes fueled the economy. He lobbied Congress for huge cuts in corporate and income taxes. The result was the 1926 Revenue Act. Mellon thought that these cuts would help all Americans, but it was wealthy Americans who benefited most. Still, the tax cuts did help the country as a whole because wealthy people had more money to put back into the economy. This extra money in the stock market and in society fueled the boom of the twenties. This boom ended with a crash when the stock market plummeted in 1929.

## Swim Style

Before World War I, women had worn bathing dresses to swim in. These elaborate outfits even included bloomers. After the war, designers showcased modern bathing suit styles. These early styles consisted of form-fitting tank tops pulled down and belted over short woolen shorts.

■ Women's swimwear in the 1920s was far from glamorous.

# Free-Spirited Fashion

The twenties was a decade of happy-go-lucky attitudes encouraged by prosperity. Women's waistlines moved from the natural waist down to between the waist and the hips—and then disappeared altogether. Clothing was loose and unrestricted, much like the lifestyles of many American women. Gone were the days of showing off curves. Boyish figures and bobbed haircuts were in style, and clothes were chosen to hide any curves. Flappers led the fashion revolution. They wore outfits that were baggy and short. The dresses were often sleeveless and their bare arms created scandals. Their stockings were turned down, exposing powdered knees.

### OXFORD BAGS

■ At many university campuses, young men were not allowed to wear knickers. To get around this restriction, many turned to Oxford bags. These pants were between 22 and 40 inches wide around the bottom. Students could wear their knickers before and after class and slip the Oxford bags over them while in class.

## MEN'S CLOSETS

■ After World War I, American men returned home to closets full of clothing they had worn as teenagers. They traded in their army fatigues and dress uniforms for the sack suit. During the day, men wore these suits with colored shirts and silk ties of various patterns. Bowler hats topped off the perfect day outfit. For evening wear, elegant twenties' men wore jackets with tails. Tuxedos were slowly gaining popularity at high-society functions. For casual wear, American men wore lace-up two-toned shoes, often in white and tan, and many wore knickers—loose-fitting short pants gathered at the knee.

## And the Winner Is...

In 1921, eight women battled for the title of Miss America. It was the first time the beauty pageant had been held. Atlantic City had little tourism after Labor Day. The pageant was seen as a way to draw more people to the city in the fall. The contest was hosted by an unlikely person—a wealthy inventor, Hudson Maxim, who had made his fortune in explosives. The Miss America pageant was explosive as well! It featured a "bathing revue," during which even the men in the orchestra wore swimsuits. Sixteen-year-old Margaret Gorman was crowned the first Miss America. While many people scoffed at the contest, it fitted well with the ideas and tastes of the Jazz Age. The following year, a total of fifty-seven cities sent women to represent them at the Miss America pageant.

## Crazy for Coco

In 1914, Coco Chanel opened a hat shop in Paris, France. By 1921, the French woman's name was associated with style and elegance. She introduced a new perfume called Chanel No. 5, which became the most successful perfume ever produced.

Chanel also introduced a line of clothing that was simple and elegant, just like her perfume. Every wealthy American woman had her closets stocked with Chanel's tweed suits, jersey blouses, trench coats, turtleneck sweaters, and her "little black dress." Chanel's suits—a collarless cardigan and a skirt—have been imitated for decades.

■ Coco Chanel's illustrious design house still exists today.

## Closing the Doors

**The passing of the immigration quota bill made it more difficult for newcomers to enter the country.**

After World War I, the U.S. began to isolate itself from the affairs of the world. This attitude caused Americans to call for restrictions on immigration. Congress passed a temporary quota bill in 1921. This was the first time the U.S. had set limits on how many people could come to the country. Quotas for different countries were established. The policy restricted the number of Asians and Europeans allowed to immigrate to 150,000. The number of immigrants of any nationality could not be higher than 3 percent of the number of foreign-born citizens of that nationality living in the country in 1910. About 70 percent of foreign-born Americans were from Germany, Britain, and Ireland. The new rules favored immigration from these countries and worked against others. The aim of the act was to stop the rising immigration from eastern and southern Europe. These immigrants were seen as a threat to the U.S. political system and to American workers' job security. The restrictions on immigration in 1921 were not enough for some Americans. Many people wanted further limitations.

Quotas were again decreased with the passing of the Immigration Act of 1924. These quotas were set according to the desirability of the immigrant. Those from northern and western Europe were thought to fit into U.S. society better than those from southern and eastern Europe. Immigration quotas of people from Great Britain, Germany, and Ireland were increased. Quotas for such countries as Russia and Italy were cut. Nearly all Asians were prohibited from entering the U.S. at all.

## Newcomers to America

Despite new restrictions on immigration to the U.S., many people from around the world wanted to become Americans. People immigrated to the U.S. for a variety of reasons. Some were fleeing war and poverty. Others came simply because they felt they would have more opportunities to succeed in the U.S. than they would in their country of origin.

The adjoining chart shows the estimated percentage of immigrants and where these newcomers came from to start a new life in the U.S. during the 1920s.

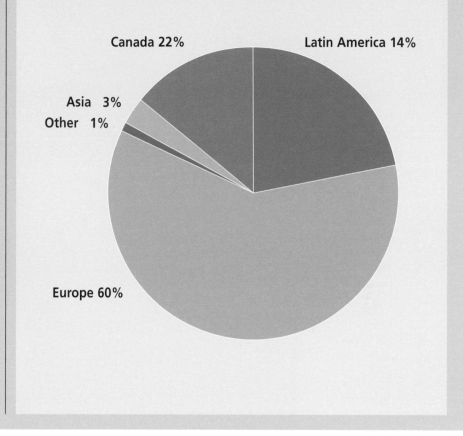

**LEGAL IMMIGRATION BETWEEN 1920–1929**

Canada 22%

Latin America 14%

Asia 3%

Other 1%

Europe 60%

## New Rules

During World War I, a limited number of Mexicans had entered the U.S. as special contract laborers. This arrangement was brought to an end in 1923, but Mexicans continued to immigrate. Mexicans arrived at the U.S. border through the 1920s when the new legislation caused European immigration to falter. Estimates place the number of Mexican immigrants as high as 500,000 during that decade alone.

■ Immigrants who arrived in the U.S. without official papers were deported.

# Empress of the Blues

Bessie Smith was one of the greatest female blues singers in history. She was known as the "Empress of the Blues" for her deep, beautiful voice. In 1923, she finished a tour of the South and went to New York to make an album. She performed with such music legends as Benny Goodman, Louis Armstrong, and James P. Johnson. Her songs "Down-Hearted Blues" and

■ Bessie Smith sold millions of albums in the 1920s.

"Gulf Coast Blues" were hits. Her unique sound and intense voice made her the most popular blues singer of the time. She earned $2,000 a week at the height of her stardom. She was the country's hottest African-American star of the twenties. As the thirties approached, people's tastes changed. They began to prefer the music of Hollywood movies and radio stars. Smith began touring the South, where she was still popular. The Empress of the Blues died in a car accident in 1937.

## THE HOT FIVES

■ Jazz trumpeter Louis Armstrong peformed with the hottest bands in Chicago when he was young. Bandleader Fletcher Henderson asked him to come to New York. Armstrong packed his bags and established himself as an incredible talent. In 1925, he started his own bands. The Hot Fives and Hot Sevens performed and recorded albums. Armstrong produced some of the best jazz ever on these albums, with classic songs such as "Cornet Chop Suey" and "West End Blues." At the same time, Armstrong and his bands challenged what people thought this style of music was.

Armstrong abandoned the old style of having a clarinet, trumpet, and trombone playing together. He introduced solos to the mix. These solos were improvised—audiences never knew what to expect from one show to the next. Armstrong's expression, creativity, and technical skill flowed from his trumpet. He introduced scat, which is singing meaningless syllables along with the jazz melodies. This technique was picked up by such jazz greats as Ella Fitzgerald. Louis Armstrong revolutionized jazz in the twenties and became a music legend in the process.

"Man, if you gotta ask, you'll never know."

Louis Armstrong's response when asked to define jazz

## Americans Experience Rhapsody

Composer George Gershwin had been working toward musical stardom for many years. At 12 years old, he was a piano genius. He soon began writing his own songs. In 1919, 21-year-old Gershwin's first Broadway production, *La La Lucille*, opened. A year later, he enjoyed his first hit song with "Swanee." With the help of singer Al Jolson, the record sold 2 million copies, along with 1 million copies of the sheet music. In 1924, Gershwin reached the next level with "Rhapsody in Blue." He had composed "Rhapsody" on the invitation of Paul Whiteman. Whiteman and his orchestra performed the piece first in New York City. A mix of harmonies, rhythms, and jazz, it brought Gershwin fame, fortune, and respect in the music industry.

Over the next few years, George and his brother Ira worked together to produce many successful Broadway shows, including *Funny Face* (1927) and *Of Thee I Sing* (1931), which was the first musical comedy to win a Pulitzer Prize.

## The Duke of Jazz

Duke Ellington began his career as a poster printer and designer in Washington, DC, but he and a small band performed at concerts and parties whenever they could. In 1923, he decided to try to make a name for himself in music in New York City. He worked for other bandleaders, but he soon formed his own group at the Hollywood Club on Broadway. His amazing talent on the piano was not what drew him attention and fame. It was his composing, arranging, and skills as a bandleader that made him a star. In 1927, Ellington and his band began performing at the Cotton Club for non-African-American audiences. In order to make this

■ Duke Ellington is one of the most influential musicians in the history of jazz.

leap, Ellington and other bandleaders had to pay a great percentage of their fees to the promoters.

In his career, Ellington composed about 2,000 pieces of music for ballets, movies, opera, and his own jazz band. He traveled all over the world to entertain audiences in more than 20,000 performances. Ellington won eleven Grammy Awards and nineteen honorary doctorate degrees. He was awarded the U.S. Presidential Medal of Freedom in 1969, and the French Legion of Honor in 1973. His long and successful music career made Ellington a jazz legend.

## Paying for Panama

In 1903, the U.S. helped Panama rebel against Colombia to become a separate country. The 1903 rebellion was spurred by the Colombian government's refusal to allow the U.S. to complete and run the Panama Canal. Panama received payment from the U.S. for this right, and it was time to pay Colombia too.

In April 1921, the U.S. Senate approved a treaty with Colombia. In the treaty, the U.S. government agreed to pay Colombia $25 million to recognize Panama's independence. Senator Henry Cabot Lodge encouraged the U.S. government to pay the sum to settle the bitterness between Colombia and the U.S. He also hoped that it would help the government negotiate drilling rights for American companies with operations in Colombia.

## Repaying World War I

In January 1921, the Allies—including Britain, France, and the U.S.—presented Germany with the bill for World War I. Germany was blamed for the war and was ordered to pay damages. The U.S. claimed the "rights and advantages" won by the Allies in the Treaty of Versailles. The U.S. would not, however, accept any responsibilities assumed by the Allies. The next step was to collect the payments from Germany. The Allies made demands, but Germany suggested lower amounts. So Allied troops entered Germany to prove they were serious about their demands.

In March, Germany reluctantly offered $32 billion to compensate the Allies for the war. This fine was higher than any country had paid ever before. The settlement depended on the agreement of the German people. The National Socialist German Workers' Party—the Nazi

■ Adolf Hitler delivers a passionate speech to German citizens.

Party—rebelled against it. They interrupted political meetings and threatened those in favor of paying the fine. In the end, Germany reduced the size of its military to 100,000 soldiers, and recognized the sovereignty of Poland, Belgium, and Czechoslovakia. It did not, however, pay the fine.

# League of Nations

On November 15, 1920, the League of Nations met for the first time. The man behind the agency, President Woodrow Wilson, was not there. He had dreamed of such an international organization that would work for peace and disarmament. Members of the League promised to respect each other's territory. If a conflict arose, the other members would help the involved parties discuss the issue and bring it to a non-violent conclusion. The U.S. government failed to pass the Treaty of Versailles, which held the League's bill. Wilson himself had encouraged senators to vote "no" because of changes to the bill made by the Republican Senator Henry Cabot Lodge.

■ The members of the League of Nations assembled in Geneva, Switzerland, on November 15, 1920.

While campaigning against the bill, Wilson suffered a stroke. Republican Warren Harding was nominated to run in the 1920 election, and he won. In his inaugural address, Harding told Americans that he would not become involved in conflicts in Europe.

## CONTROL OF NICARAGUA

■ The U.S. had been involved in Nicaragua since the turn of the century. For the first part of the 1900s, the U.S. supported a conservative government in Nicaragua. U.S. marines were stationed there to protect the government from a **coup**. As long as a conservative government was in place, U.S. businesses were protected.

In the early 1920s, the U.S. government wanted to make Nicaragua more secure so that the marines could pull out. It trained a professional military to guarantee fair elections and keep order in the country. The elections brought a weak government into power in 1925. The marines left and civil war broke out. When the defeated Conservative candidate, General Emiliano Chamorro, took over the government, the U.S. forced him from office. Adolfo Díaz, the former Conservative president, then took over. In 1927, after much civil unrest, thousands of marines landed in Nicaragua to support Díaz's government. The marines stayed in Nicaragua until 1933. When they left, they passed the responsibilities to the U.S.-trained National Guard. American involvement in Nicaragua strained U.S.–Latin American relations for decades.

# Where Did It Happen?

Match each number with an event:

a) Red Grange's professional football city

b) Location of the Monkey Trial

c) Namesake of a major scandal

d) Site of the first commercial radio broadcast

e) Charles Lindbergh's starting point

f) Host city of the Miss America pageant

g) City to which the Saint Francis Dam supplied water

h) First U.S. team to join National Hockey League

i) Site of statewide floods

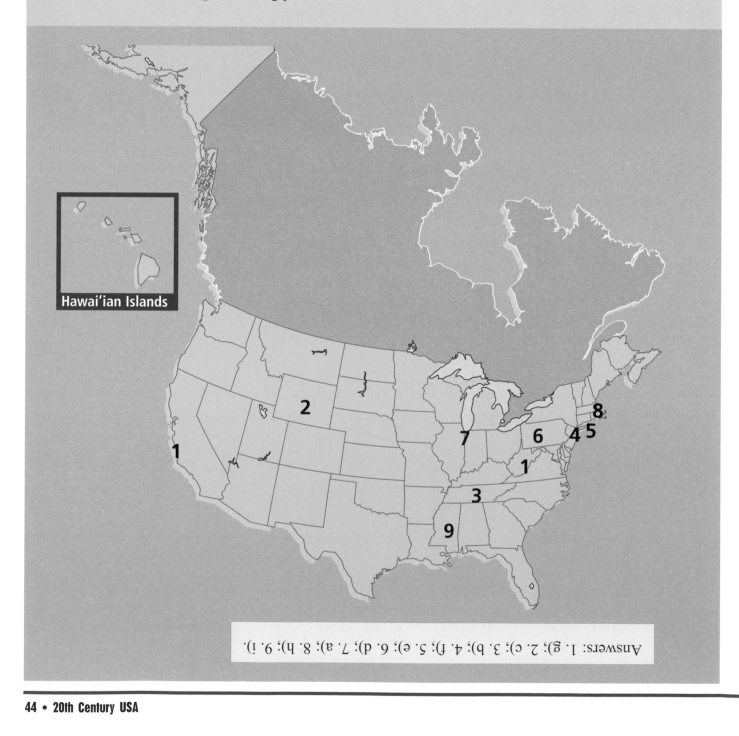

Hawai'ian Islands

Answers: 1. g); 2. c); 3. b); 4. f); 5. e); 6. d); 7. a); 8. h); 9. i).

Activities

## True or False

**1.** The U.S. suffered a brief recession before the boom in the twenties.

**2.** Harry Houdini credited supernatural powers for his feats.

**3.** During the twenties, India's Mohandas Gandhi was jailed for encouraging people to rebel against authority.

**4.** Gene Sarazen was the first golfer to win the four major tournaments of the time.

**5.** Margaret Gorman was the first Miss America.

Answers:
1. True
2. False. He did not believe in supernatural powers.
3. True
4. True
5. True

## Newsmakers

Match the following names with his or her claim to fame:

5. taught evolution in school

6. invented the crossword puzzle

1. involved in Teapot Dome scandal

7. fashion designer

2. Pulitzer Prize winner

8. aviator

3. invented iron lung

9. Treasury secretary

4. bodybuilding legend

10. wrote *The Great Gatsby*

a) Philip Drinker
b) Charles Atlas
c) Albert Bacon Fall
d) John T. Scopes
e) Edith Wharton
f) Gregory Hartswick
g) Charles Lindbergh
h) Andrew W. Mellon
i) F. Scott Fitzgerald
j) Coco Chanel

Answers: 1 c); 2 e); 3 a); 4. b); 5 d); 6. f); 7. j); 8. g); 9. h); 10. i).

**affiliation:** close connection with

**ad-libbed:** made up on the spot

**anarchists:** people who want to rebel against the government

**bootleggers:** people who sell alchohol illegally

**caddy:** person who carries a golfer's clubs

**controversial:** disputed

**corruption:** dishonesty

**coup:** the sudden and forceful overthrowing of a government

**dominion:** a self-governing country within the Commonwealth

**deported:** forcibly removed from the country

**ethics:** moral principles

**exiled:** sent away from one's country as punishment

**fascist:** one who believes in extreme dictatorial government

**flapper:** a young woman who rebelled against norms in the 1920s.

**foreclosed:** took back property because of unpaid loans

**front:** in war, the place where two sides are fighting

**inciting:** stirring to action

**indicted:** formally accused of serious legal wrongdoing

**levees:** embankments formed or put up to stop a river from flooding

**prism:** a transparent item that separates white light into colors.

**repealing:** officially canceling

**slapstick:** comedy full of rough play and action rather than words

**speakeasies:** bars selling illegal liquor

**sucker-punched:** punched when the receiver does not see it coming

**vaudeville:** entertainment made up of many different acts

Here are some book resources and Internet links if you want to learn more about the people, places, and events that made headlines during the 1920s.

## Books

Brewster, Todd, and Peter Jennings. *The Century for Young People*. New York: Random House, 1999.

Estrin, Jack C. *American History Made Simple*. New York: The Stonesong Press, 1991.

Grant, John. *Encyclopedia of Walt Disney's Animated Characters*. New York: Hyperion, 1993.

Sabuda, Robert. *Tutankhamen's Gift*. New York: Maxwell Macmillan International, 1994.

## Internet Links

http://xroads.virginia.edu/~HYPER/Allen/ch03.html

http://www.louisville.edu/~kprayb01/1920s.html

http://silent-movies.com

http://www.btinternet.com/~dreklind/threetwo/Jazzhome.htm

For information about other U.S. subjects, type your key words into a search engine such as Alta Vista or Yahoo!